MAP.
FEB. 1998.

HIDDE HALBERTSMA

THE VINTAGE CAR DIARY

REBO PRODUCTIONS

J A N U A R Y

Inset: 3-litre Bentley Speed (1926), four cylinders, 2,996 cc, 85 h.p. The 3-litre was the first car designed by the famous British maker Walter Owen Bentley. It was built from 1921 to 1929. The different versions can be recognised by the colour of the radiator badge. This 'red label' indicates the 'Speed' model with coachwork by Vandenplas. The top speed was around 103 m.p.h. (165 k.p.m).

1935 Mercedes-Benz 500K
(acrylic by Huub Lepelaar)

From horse and cart to the car

Although the first motor cars with internal combustion engines were built and sold by the Germans Daimler (1885) and Benz (1886), the French influence on the development of the motor car in the early years was considerable. The speed record was held by a French driver in a French car until 1905. Prior to the First World War, the most important innovations in the automobile industry originated in France. Some words from the French car industry have passed into international usage, such as chassis and chauffeur.

01

02

The Spijker Landaulette is a conflict in styles. The automobile age has clearly dawned and with it the beginning of the true development of the car, yet much has been retained from the coaching era.

Before the arrival of the motor car people mainly travelled by horse and cart, in a carriage, or on foot. The Landaulette coach was a variant of the classic Landau. The Landaulette had a folding roof with a glass screen between the coachman, who sat outside, and his passengers who either sat on a bench seat at the rear or, if necessary, on a folding seat. This Spijker Landaulette from 1924 mirrors the Landaulette coach. The driver sat outside with the passengers inside on the bench seat or folding seats. Spijker was not the only company to make this type of vehicle.

A 1902 Holsman Rambler with two cylinder, 1,045 cc engine that delivered 5 h.p. The Holsman Automobile Company existed from 1902 to 1909. Cars from this time do not resemble modern day automobiles. The influence of the coachbuilder is obvious in the design of this 'high-wheeler', with the driver still seated on a buckboard.

The Mille Miglia.
The spectators at this historic race could be from half a century ago. The black and white photograph of the Mercedes looks fifty years old yet it was taken in 1986 – black and white can be deceptive. The second picture is almost identical but in colour.

This eight cylinders Alfa Romeo 8C 2300 also took part in the 1986 Mille Miglia. This car won the race in 1932.

The Mille Miglia

Before the war there were a number of major competitions – all organised with the intention of testing the reliability and endurance of the cars that took part to the extreme. The Monte Carlo Rally is one of the few of these events remaining. One race that vanished as a result of highway improvements was the Italian Mille Miglia (or 1000 miles race) . It was run between 1927 and 1957. In the 1980s the race was reborn for veteran cars of the era. The spectacular event lasts for four days including registration, scrutinising and prize giving. The cars are chosen for both their sporting and historical background. Spectators can enjoy watching many unique classic cars, including some that won the Mille Miglia, Le Mans, or Monte Carlo Rally.

'History is more or less bunk...'
(Henry Ford (1863-1947)

A Model-A Ford from about 1928. In 1921, Ford sold at least half of the cars in the United States. Henry Ford seemed hidebound by the enormously successful Model-T, but gave in to pressure from his son Edsel Bryant Ford to develop a new car with an air-cooled engine: the Model-A. When the Model-A replaced the Model-T, the entire manufacturing plant had to be changed, with a loss of five month's production. Although the Model-A was very successful, Ford's competitors were very active in those five lost months. Once production restarted, Ford's status had changed from the key player in the industry to just another formidable competitor.

09 10 11 12

Ford (United States)

The automobile plant of Henry Ford (1863-1947) was made famous through his Model-T Ford. It was the first standard model in history to be produced on a production line. Ford's name became famous for his cars but also synonymous with mass production. His success was founded upon keen price setting and a fundamentally sound vehicle. Little variety was available: Henry Ford became known for offering the Model-T in "any colour – so long as it's black." The Model-T can be said to have created mobility in the United States, because more then 15,000,000 of them were sold. This was only exceeded by the VW Beetle.

13 14

15 16

The 1927 Model-A Ford superseded the Model-T. The four cylinder, 3,300 cc motor delivered 40 h.p. In contrast to the Model-T that was virtually unchanged after the original design, the Model-A underwent modification virtually every year. Since that time, the annual alteration of models has become characteristic of the American auto industry.

17 18

Cadillac (United States)

Detroit is 'Motown' – the city in the United States that builds motor cars. General Motors, Chrysler, and Ford are all based in Detroit. The city was founded in 1710 by the French Marquis Antoine de la Mothe CADILLAC. His name subsequently adorned a respected make of car. Cadillac was originally founded as the Henry Ford Company but Ford quit the company in 1902 and the name was changed to Cadillac. This famous make is responsible for a number of important milestones such as the electric self-starter (1912), the synchronised gearbox (1928), and power-assisted steering (1954).

19

20

21

22

23

24

A 1954 Cadillac with the typical elongated lines of the 1950s.

The noble emblem of the Cadillac was inspired by the aristocratic origins of the Marquis de la Mothe Cadillac, from whom the name was is derived.

Cadillac 1954. Cadillac had its own styling department from 1925, ensuring the cars continuously retained their own distinctive style.

MG (Great Britain)

'Morris Garages' was started in 1913 by W.R. Morris and changed its name to 'Morris Motors Ltd.' in 1919. The factory manager Kimber started to modify standard Morris cars which he called M.G. from the abbreviation of the company name. The MG Car Company was formed as a separate company in 1928.

This photograph offers a splendid overview of the post-war MG sports car. From left to right we can see an MG TD (1951), an MG A (1960), an MG B (1963), and an MG Midget (1971). Note the development of the radiator grill from tall and vertical to low and horizontal.

Hispano Suiza (France)

Hispano Suiza, as the name suggests, is of Spanish and Swiss origins. The business was founded at a factory in Barcelona in 1904 by a Swiss Engineer called Marc Birkigt. By 1911, the cars were already being assembled in France. The company mainly built cars, although they also produced aero engines during the First World War. Cars were also made in Britain, the United States, and France under licence. The company did not survive the 1940s. The French factory closed in 1939 and the last Hispano Suiza rolled out of the Spanish factory in 1944.

1928 Hispano Suiza H6B Roadster. The famous H6B Roadster was introduced in 1919 by the French Hispano Suiza factory. The very powerful car was one of the best cars in the world with a six cylinder in-line engine of 6,597cc, delivering 135 h.p.

1933 MG J2. MG started building sports cars before the war. Their post war popularity knew no bounds.

FEBRUARY

Ferrari F40
(acrylic by Huub Lepelaar)

1902 Panhard & Levassor. Panhard & Levassor were important car makers at the turn of the nineteenth and twentieth centuries. Racing cars of this make were usually among the leading cars at all important races from 1894 onwards.

The DAF 600 at first only flourished in The Netherlands. DAF success abroad followed the 1962 Monte Carlo Rally, when six of the seven DAF 750s taking part completed the gruelling rally.

DAF (The Netherlands)

DAF started as a machine works in 1928 and moved on to building cars via the production of trailers. Today DAF produce only trucks. Between 1958 and 1972 DAF also sold private cars which were equipped with an unusual transmission system – the Variomatic. This is an automatic transmission with a continuously variable drive ratio, achieved by a V-belt that runs between rollers. The effective radius of the rollers adjusts to engine speed and torque.

The first DAF car in 1959 was the DAF 600. The other models can almost be counted on the fingers of one hand – the DAF 750, the Daffodil, and the DAF 33, 44, and 55. The final model was the DAF 66. DAF built a factory at Born in The Netherlands in 1972 in conjunction with Volvo. In 1976, the production of cars passed wholly to Volvo and the final DAF 66 cars were sold as Volvos. A point of interest is that the Volvo 343 was originally developed as the DAF 88.

A 1972 DAF 33 with air-cooled 747 cc opposed twin cylinder engine. The DAF was particularly successful with motorists who had problem changing gear. This included many older women, leading to various uncomplimentary epithets being directed at the marque. Today, the DAF is a sought after collector's car. The DAF owner's club in The Netherlands has some 1,800 members.

01 02 03 04

05 06 07 08

The Auburn/Duessenberg/Cord company was facing serious problems in 1937. The sportive Cord 812 was to save the company but the attempt failed , resulting in bankruptcy. The 4,730 cc, eight cylinder motor delivered 190 h.p. The Cord was one of the first American cars with front-wheel drive.

The distinctive lines of the Cord 812 were designed by Gordon Buehrig. It is one of the most eye-catching designs from the 1930s.

1961 Skoda Felicia

The first suggestion of 'wings' can be seen clearly on this 1956 Oldsmobile Holiday. The lavish use of chrome, spacious design, and big engine are typical of the late 1950s in the United States. This trend is in direct contrast to the European tendency for less ostentatious design. This Oldsmobile Holiday has a 5,309 cc V-8 engine giving 220 h.p.

Amalgamation of different makes of car had started in the United States before the First World War. Buick, Oldsmobile, and Oakland were brought together by W.C. Durant under the General Motors name. Chevrolet was added later. This concentration led to mass production which slowly drove the more exclusive marques from the market.

Buick was also part of the General Motors Company. This brochure for the Buick Roadmaster 76C Convertible (the V-8 engine delivered 200 h.p.) portrayed not just the powerful car. The couple standing next to the car embody the 'American dream'. The Buick is represented as the essential fulfilment of that dream.

09 10

11 12

13 14

15 16

17 18

19 20

Rover started life in 1903 by making motorcycles. Within a year though they started to build light cars. The company has made beautiful, stylish cars of classic British design for as long as can be remembered. This 3.5 litre Rover from 1973 is a fine example of the marque.

This early Austin is an example of the craftsmanship of British designers.

21	22	23
24	25	26
27	28	29

1973 3.5 litre Rover. The emblem of the marque portrays an ancient Viking ship, The Dragon, to suggest a roving adventurer.

M A R C H

Morris Mini-Cooper
(acrylic by Huub Lepelaar)

Spijker

Spijker was the marque of the first large Dutch car manufacturer – N.V. Trompenberg. which was founded in 1902. The company gained international recognition through its second place in the famous 1907 Peking–Paris run.

1911 Spijker Runabout with 18 h.p., 2,798 cc four cylinder engine. Spijker launched 16 and 18 h.p. models at the 1910 Paris motor show. Both cars had very modern, compact engines for the times. The cylinder block was founded as one piece and the car had the three pedals we are accustomed to today – brake, accelerator, and clutch – except that the accelerator was centrally positioned.

Right:
1911 Spijker runabout. Spijker did not just make cars. Around 1910, they could also deliver trucks, ambulances, buses, and fire engines.

Lombard Racer type GA-IR of 1927. The four cylinder 1,093 cc motor delivered 45 h.p., giving this racing car a top speed of 100 m.p.h. (160 k.p.h.)

A Citroën Traction Avant Berline 11 Sport (1937) with the typical Citroën grill.

Traction Avant Berline Sport from 1937 with four cylinder 1,911cc engine. To the left of the Traction Avant is a Citroën Commerciale of 1936.

Citroën Traction Avant

The great breakthrough of the Traction Avant was made by Citroën in 1933. The development of the front suspension cost so much, and the car was so complex, that Citroën would have gone to the wall without financial support from the Michelin family. In addition to front wheel drive, the monocoque body was unique at that time. The Traction Avant was made in various versions until 1957.

1939 Citroën Traction Avant, four cylinders, 1,628cc, 56 h.p.

To get in to the Renault KZ2, one first had to step over the foot high (25cm) running board.

Riding in a pre-war automobile was quite different to our modern cars. The Renault KZ2 is a good example. The seating was nowhere near as comfortable as present day seats. Folding seats were often fixed to the side panels and there were no safety belts.

The double declutch

Following its introduction by Cadillac in 1928, more and more cars were made with synchromesh gearboxes. Without synchromesh, the driver had to use the technique to change down known as double declutch. The VW Beetle was delivered after the war without synchromesh (it cost about £160/$250 as an optional extra). The sound of grating gears from bad gear changes continued to be heard for many more years as a result.

The driving position of a Renault KZ2. During the 1920s, the position of the pedals (brake, clutch, and accelerator) was gradually standardised.

A Franklin 18B Olympic of 1933; the six cylinder 4,493 cc, air-cooled engine delivered 100 h.p.

09 10 11

12 13 14

15 16 17

The 'double declutch' worked as follows:
push in the clutch; set the gear to neutral; let out the clutch; press accelerator to bring the revolutions of the engine up to the same level as the propeller shaft; depress the clutch; select the gear; let out the clutch again.

Green lamella in the radiator grill denotes green interior trim.

Note the illuminated number plate.

MG TD (1951), 1,250cc. This nostalgic model in ivory harks back strongly to its predecessors – the MG TC of 1945 and even the MG TA of 1936. Yet this is a much more technologically advanced sports car than the TC, with a 1,250cc engine and luxurious accessories such as a heater. The lamella of the delightful grill should match the colour of the leather seating and trim – in this case dark green. The windscreen can be lowered and side windows are available for cold weather.

CLEVELAND
SHELL
MOTOR OIL
GARGOYLE
Mobiloil
"C"
Castrol
MOTORINE
GARGOYLE
Mobiloil
BB
JUNIOR SHELL
JOHN BULL
Castrol
DUBARRY'S
TALCUM POWDER
Castrol

BODEN
BGT
special
DRAAIENDE TROMMEL NIET AANRAKEN
VOLVO
VOLVO
VW 1600
1000

Small collectors

The purchase, restoration, and maintenance of veteran and classic cars is expensive and therefore not possible for everyone. Some people with less money to spend collect parts and motoring paraphernalia.

Some enthusiasts are interested in old oil cans and have been known to assemble impressive collections.

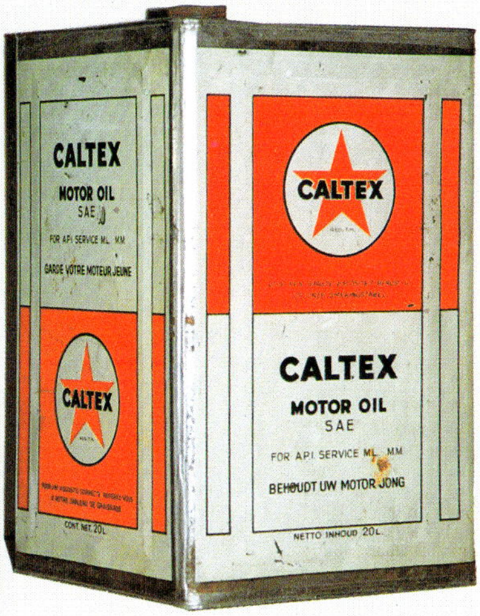

Knave plates (often incorrectly called hub caps) from Dodge and Mercedes. These wheel embellishments from old cars are much sought after. Lucy Pearson from the United States has the largest collection. She has collected 140,000 over the years. Lucy sells duplicates from her collection and most clients find what they want from her.

There is also considerable interest among collectors in marque and model emblems.

24 25 26 27 28 29 30 31

A P R I L

1902 Opel Daracq
(acrylic by Huub Lepelaar)

Inset: this 1938 Alfa Romeo 8C 2900B took part in the 1986 Mille Miglia.

Sports cars

British sports cars acquired widespread popularity immediately after the war. They sold extremely well in the United States, where there was intense competition between MG, Jaguar, Triumph, and Austin Healey.

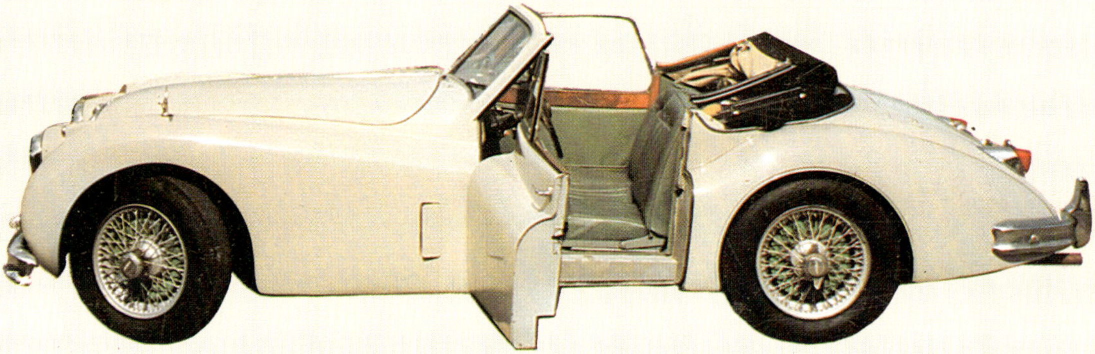

The XK140 Jaguar is the predecessor of the famous E type.

Reverse trade with the United States: the sports cars on this transporter – including a Triumph TR2 and a pair of MGs –are headed back to Europe.

More than eighty per cent of the Austin Healeys produced were for the American market.

The lines of the MG A make every sports car enthusiast's heart beat faster. MG was also a strong player in the American market.

01

02

03

04

05

06

07

08

09

10

The 1926 Bugatti 35a Tecla. Instead of a straight configuration for the eight cylinders, they were arranged in two blocks of four cylinders. Their 1,991cc delivered 90 h.p. and a top speed for this 'Grand Prix' car of 94 m.p.h. (150 k.p.h.)

Bugatti

The Italian Ettore Bugatti (1881–1947) was a brilliant designer and constructor. Starting in 1902, he worked in England and France (for Peugeot among others). In 1909 he set up as an independent car maker in Molsheim (Alsace-Lorraine). From here he introduced one technical breakthrough after another. His cars stood apart because of the innovative design of both the overall car and the small details.

11

12

Following the appealing success of his racing cars, there was a demand for a fast but comfortable touring car. Bugatti met this by introducing his type 57 in 1934. The 3,256 cc eight cylinder motor has a power of 135 h.p.

Speed fanatics

Speed is in the blood of Italian car makers. The country has produced many constructors of successful racing and sports cars: Alfa Romeo, Ferrari, Lancia, Maserati, Fiat, Lamborghini… even Bugatti was Italian in origin.

This Pininfarina-designed Alfa 1900 Coupé has the racing pedigree for success in motor sport.

Lamborghini Maiura

13

14

15

16

17

18

19

20

This racing freak – or racing cigar – is an early Alfa Romeo. The Italian owner is very proud of his acquisition and busy restoring the car.

Citroën (France)

André Citroën founded his own works in 1919. He mass produced cars from the very start. By 1925 he was the largest car manufacturer in Europe, making 500 cars every day and the company remained the largest volume manufacturer in Europe until 1950. Citroën's strength lay in the long runs of their mass produced cars.

The Citroën emblem on the grill of a 1936 Commerciale 74. The logo was derived from the 'Chevron' bevelled teeth of gears and cogs that was André Citroën's original product range.

A 1923 Citroën Type C Two-seater, which was nicknamed 'The Clover Leaf'. This two-seater was enormously successful. Between 1922 and 1926 some 75,000 of these cars were made. They had a four cylinder 856cc engine delivering 11 h.p. that could reach 38 m.p.h. (60 k.p.h.).

21

22

Citroën 2CV (1959), twin cylinders, 425cc. Citroën started worked as early as 1930 on the development of the 2CV. The car was not launched until 1948. The power unit is a simple air-cooled opposed twin cylinder engine. To provide taxation advantages, the power of the 'Deux Chevaux' was very limited. In the course of its life, its power was increased and so were the number of accessories. It is however the simplicity of the 2CV that led to its popularity.

Renault won the World Rally Championship with the Renault 4 Alpine in 1973.

Renault 4 Alpine. In the 1960s, the designer Jean Rédélé fitted a sports car body to a Renault 4CV, resulting in the A110. The car was developed further as the S and 1800 series, which won many motor sport prizes between 1969 and 1978.

23

24

25

26

27

28

29

30

MAY

1935 Mark I Jaguar
(acrylic by Huub Lepelaar)

Car clubs

There is an enormous variety in car clubs. They may be general motoring clubs or for cars from a particular marque. Some clubs are for enthusiasts of a specific type of car. There are for example more than one MG owners clubs. These organise rallies, treasure hunts, and other competitions, but also provide advice and support on restoration and tracing of spare parts. Enthusiasts talk ten to the dozen at their meetings about their shared love for their veteran or classic cars.

01

05

MG races at Zandvoort circuit in 1990.

Bottom right: the 'Gullwing' 300 SL is one of the finest Mercedes-Benz to ever leave the drawing board. The Gullwing, with its winged doors, was exhibited as an experimental model in 1952, with a six cylinde 3 litre engine. The car won a number of races for Mercedes-Benz, including the 1953 Le Mans 24 hour race.

A club day for the German classic Alfa Romeo club.

02 03 04

06 07 08

GTV day in The Netherlands at Doorwerth Castle near Arnhem, for the Alfa Guilia Bertone 'Register'. This club is specifically for owners of Bertone designed Alfa Romeo GTVs.

Porsche (Germany)

Porsche was founded in Stuttgart in 1938. It was not until ten years later that the company began to design and build its own motor cars. They decided to specialise in luxury sports cars. The characteristic rounded lines of the Porsche have hardly changed over the years. The firm established its reputation in the years after the war and is equated with the likes of Jaguar and Ferrari. The spirit of Ferdinand von Porsche lives on in the cars that bear his name.

1964 Porsche 356C. There are similarities between the Porsche 356 and Volkswagen, which was also the creation of Ferdinand von Porsche. An example is the cable operated brakes of the VW Beetle. The trailing arms front suspension harks back to an earlier patent of Ferdinand von Porsche that he used for the 1934 16 cylinder Grand Prix Auto Union.

The double rear window of this Beetle indicates that it is a Standard type 1/11 with 1,131cc engine that was built under British management. The rear windows led to the 'Spectacles Beetle' nickname. In March 1953 the window became oval and then rectangular in 1957.

Volkswagen Beetle (Germany)

The history of the Beetle starts in June 1934 when Ferdinand von Porsche had the idea for the car. The car was shown in public in 1938 as the VW38. It was also exhibited abroad and a journalist in New York jokingly said it looked like a 'Beetle', sparking a name was to stick. The original intention was that Germans should pay DM 5 per week but few were delivered because of the outbreak of war. After the war the British, who occupied that part of Germany, established production and subsequently the Germans themselves developed the car. The last German-made Beetle left the production line in 1978. Since then some 20,000 more were made every year for many years in Mexico. Eventually 21 million Beetles were made.

A 1964 Porsche 356C. The timeless, beautiful rounded lines of the Porsche originate from 1958. Since the shape of the 356 changed little over the years, it can easily be mistaken for an older car.

09 10 11 12

13 14 15 16

The Beetle only achieved its cult status towards the end of the 1980s. This fine 1965 VW Beetle was restored in 1996.

With MG too there was considerable attention to detail...

17

18

1924 Spijker C4 Convertible; six cylinders, 5,742cc, 35 h.p. The car was designed in 1920 by the aircraft and automotive engineer Frits Koolhoven, who joined Spijker at the beginning of the Twenties. From 1924 until 1940 he had his own aircraft factory. The six cylinder engine originated from the German company Maybach and the car had a robust body. The car performed well and was known for the quality and thoroughness of its construction. The only point on which this convertible did not match its competitors was its lack of four wheel braking. The subsequent introduction of all-wheel braking in 1923 was unable to save the company which failed in 1925.

Right: Ferrari 275 GTB. Enzo Ferrari never regarded himself as a manufacturer. He said he considered himself craftsman with the hands. Attention to detail is as essential in the design and building of each supercar as in the hand crafting of some beautiful object. This is why every Ferrari is such a work of art.

This small 1967 Alfa 1300 GT is the junior sister of the Alfa Guilia Super 1600. The wide dark radiator grill caused the car to be dubbed 'the post box'.

19

20

21

22

23

24

Leyat (France)

The development of the car led to some very extravagant and strange variations. During the first decades of its development, no standards had been established. The Parisian Leyat was inspired in 1922 by aircraft. The resulting car looked as though he had mounted the cockpit from a single-engined aircraft on wheels – although most planes at that time had open cockpits. The beast had a wooden body and propeller and weighed a mere 250 kg. The twin cylinder engine gave the Helicar a top speed of 62 m.p.h (100 k.p.h.). Although the propeller had a protective guard, the Helicar must have been a considerable danger on the road.

25

1910 Maxwell Briscoe

26

27

28

Alfa Guilietta Berlina

29

30

31

The 1922 Leyat Helicar looked as though the Frenchman Leyat had scrapped a single-engined aircraft and put it on wheels. The Helicar had a top speed of 62 m.p.h. (100 k.p.h.). Only one example was built by Leyat and its first owner was Jean-Jacques Peugeot.

Within its fine rounded lines, this sporty Porsche 356 has the considerable power waiting to be turned into high speed that has become synonymous with Porsche.

J U N E

Inset: the famous Renault emblem, mounted here on a 1925 KZ2. Renault has shaped the history of the motor car. Its founder, Louis Renault, invented the transmission system of propeller shaft-rear axle-differential still in use today. In 1914, 600 Renault Paris taxis carried soldiers to the front line to save France by stemming the advance of the Germans towards the Marne. Over the years the company has introduced many famous models. Today it is one of the two giants of the French car industry, the other being Peugeot.

1929 Hispano Suiza H6B
(acrylic by Huub Lepelaar)

De Dion-Bouton et Cie. (France)

The Frenchman Bouton originally made toys. From model steam engines, he changed to steam vehicles on the initiative of the investor Count De Dion. De Dion-Bouton introduced a three-wheeler with an air-cooled single cylinder engine in 1895. The engines of that time from Benz and Daimler turned no faster than 500 to 900 revolutions per minute but De Dion-Bouton turned over at 1,500 r.p.m. The engine design was so good that other manufacturers copied its inventions. An example is the power source of the first Harley-Davidson, which was really just a cycle with an auxiliary motor. This was made from blueprints of the De Dion-Bouton engine and is therefore an example of industrial espionage.

The 1898 De Dion-Bouton Quadricycle with a single cylinder 285cc engine that developed 2,25 h.p. The company started with tricycles. By 1896 they changed over to making four-wheelers, the quadricycle. In 1902, with a monthly production of 200 cars, they were even the world's largest car maker. Their hay-days were before the First World War. After the war the company began a gradual decline and was put into liquidation in 1932.

01 02 03

06 07 08

Eighty per cent of the production of Austin Healeys were destined for the American market. The Austin Healey 3000 Mk 3 sold extremely well; in four years 17,712 were built. A change in US law meant they could no longer be sold in America which brought about the marque's demise.

When the success of the Traction Avant began to fade, Citroën launched the Citroën DS with its revolutionary design in 1955. The car set new standards for transmission and gearbox technology and also for suspension.

04

05

09

10

This 1972 Citroën DS21 has a four cylinder 1,911cc engine of 93 horse power with front-wheel drive. The suspension has high-pressure pneumatic parts which were then unique. The suspension height could even be increased for rough terrain.

An unusual pair: a 1969 Mark II Daimler and a 1973 Volvo 1800.

June

11

12

13

15

16

Before the Second World War, Alfa Romeo built legendary sports cars. This Alfa has a body by an unknown builder – probably Castagna – on a RLSS chassis. This Super Sports is very similar to the Mercedes that was immensely popular at the time.

Steam cars

During the early years of the motor car, the competition between the steam engine and internal combustion motor was far from decided. In the final 25 years of the nineteenth century steam cars were volume produced in factories. The big disadvantage of steamers was the time taken to heat the water. The reasonable road network but poor train service in France, made these cars very popular there. The cumbersome problem of stoking was done away with in 1888 by the introduction of oil burners to heat the water.

Eventually the internal combustion engine gained the upper hand and the steam car stopped being made in Europe in 1907. The last steam car was made in the United States in 1934, which is less peculiar than it may seem due to the fact that in 1926 an ordinary petrol driven car could not exceed 62 m.p.h. (100 k.p.h.) whilst a steam car managed 94 m.p.h. (150 k.p.h.).

Luxury

Travelling in the early motor cars was not particularly luxurious. Gradually, improvements were made in comfort for both driver and passengers. Some of those improvements were the introduction by Blériot, in 1904, of a heater, an electric starter on a 1912 Cadillac – so that the car no longer had to be hand cranked – and the first cars with electric windscreen wipers, which appeared in the United States in 1923.

14

17

18

19

20

This Duesenberg exudes pure luxury.

The MG Midget: Tom Thumb in seven league boots.

The sight of two Ferrari GTEs together is unusual. Even rarer, is that one of them from the early Sixties is not painted Ferrari red.

Austin Healey (Great Britain)

Before the war, Donald Healey worked as technical director for Triumph. He built two prototype sports cars after the war with three engineers he got to know during the war. Because he could not compete with Jaguar's XK 120, Healey sought the support of BMC. The result was the Austin Healey 100 of which the first production model left the factory in 1952. It was the first in a series of popular sports cars.

The advertising brochure for the Austin Healey Sprite – the sportive look is typically British. According to the brochure, the Sprite was available in modest colours: these were dark red, off white, light blue, beige, and olive green.

21 22 23

24 25 26 27

28 29 30

The Austin Healey is still fairly widespread and can be seen regularly at auctions and enthusiasts days. The white car is an Austin Healey 3000 Mk 2. The dark red car is a Sprite.

JULY

1932 Bugatti T55 Coupé
(acrylic by Huub Lepelaar)

Inset: Austin is a British marque that for decades made cars with typical British design. From all these fine cars – think for example of the Austin Healey and the Austin Mini – it is clear the designers had an eye for details. This emblem from a 1952 Austin A30 saloon that is unfortunately in poor condition is a fine example of such detail.

Apart from a small number of variations in the interior, the Alfa Romeo Giulia 2000 closely resembles the 1750 Saloon.

01

02

This Traction Avant has had every individual part removed. The parts will all be restored or replaced where necessary. The restoration will take considerable time but the result will be impressive.

Although it looks a hopeless case, even this Jaguar Mk II will be restored. Because such cars command high prices, many restorers find it worthwhile constructing virtually a new car provided they have the chassis with its original number.

It is difficult to assess how long restoration will take. During the work many unforeseen problems arise . The search for replacement parts is time consuming. This Austin Healey 100/6 had a completely misshapen and twisted front end following an accident. A summary of the necessary work gives some impression of what is demanded in the restoration a classic car.

The present owner initially took the car apart completely; photographs were made of each detail for reference; the chassis was pulled straight using hydraulic equipment – this has to be done to the nearest millimetre or parts will no longer fit; the chassis was then sandblasted and treated to prevent rust; the bodywork was panel beaten to remove dents and the car was reassembled to make sure everything fitted; this was followed by the rebuilding of the front axle, rear axle and propeller shaft, followed by refitting the radiator and rewiring the car. The car could then be finally put back together.

03

04

05

06

07

08

Saab (Sweden)

Saab, which was founded in 1937, built military aircraft before the Second World War. After the war it was clear Government orders would be much lower so the company sought new products. They decided to make a small car. The first model was the Saab 92. It was obvious that the designers had used wind tunnels from the outset. This resulted in the following Saab models (Saab 93, 96, 99 and 900) strongly resembling their predecessor. From the start the cars had front wheel drive and were designed for the harsh Swedish climate. In addition to these series, Saab also made four models of the Saab Sonett between 1966 and 1974.

This Saab 96 GL graces a Saab dealer's showroom to attract customers. Its beautiful lines sometimes gain more attention than newer models.

09

10

The Saab 96 qualities are regarded by many enthusiasts as outstanding. The famous rally driver Erik Carlsson tested this model for Saab. His nickname was 'roll-over' Carlsson!

1959 Buick Invicta Estate car in Magic Mirror Shalimar Blue, two-seat version, with optional child's third seat.

11

12

13

14

15

16

The grill of this EB112 is based on the old Bugatti designs.

17

18

Bugatti EB112. At the end of the 1980s an attempt was made to bring back the Bugatti. The initiative was not successful. Only one model, the EB110 was launched on the market. The EB112 unlikely to proceed beyond the prototype stage. The factory is poised on the brink of a chasm and it is uncertain whether rescue is possible.

Many enthusiasts for veteran and classic cars have a definite preference for the elegant power of the Daimler.

19

20

21

22

23

24

The Citroën DS had the irreverent nickname of 'flat iron'.

Triumph TR3. In answer to the strong sales success of MG, Triumph introduced the TR series in 1950. The TR3 and TR3A models were made between 1955 and 1962. This American TR3 is in immaculate condition.

Triumph (Great Britain)

Triumph was one of the many British car makers that had difficulties between the two wars. Immediately before the start of the second war, this became serious. Despite this, the company made a number of successful models. One of their designers was Donald Healey who gave his name after the war to the Austin Healey.
The company eventually went bust in 1939 and was bought by a Sheffield steel factory. After the war Triumph staged a come back. It lived on through exploiting the interest in British sports cars in the American market.

25

26

27

28

29

30

31

AUGUST

Alfa Romeo 6C 1750GS
(acrylic by Huub Lepelaar)

Inset: Rolls Royce was founded in 1905 by the racing driver C.S. Rolls (he won the Mille Miglia among other races) and the toolmaker F.H. Royce. This is a 1927 Rolls Royce Twenty Barker Coupé. The six cylinder 3,127 cc engine delivers 21,5 h.p. The car was a competitor for the extremely successful Hispano Suiza H6B. The famous Flying Lady mascot is mounted on the radiator. This mascot was first fitted to the radiator of Lord Montagu of Beaulieu's Silver Ghost and represents his much valued secretary.

Fiat launched the Topolino 500 in 1936. From this was derived a series of 500s that continued in production until well after the Second World War.

Fiat also made an estate car version of the 500.

01

02

03

04

05

The Volvo 1800 is a rare car. To see two of them parked together is extremely uncommon.

Volvo (Sweden)

The respectable tradition of Swedish cars rests on the shoulders of Saab and Volvo. Although Volvo (Latin for 'I roll') was founded in 1926, it did not start to make cars until the 1940s. Before this they concentrated on making trucks.

06

07

Before the war Fiat created a sensation with a small car with a modest cylinder capacity. It was the Fiat 501 (1919-1926) which had a 1,460 cc, 25 h.p. engine.

August

A 1937 Ford V8. The 3,200cc eight cylinder engine delivers 85 h.p. The recession in the Thirties were difficult times for the motor industry. Many companies failed, joined forces with other companies or were swept up by the bigger companies. Helped by its use of the V8 engine, Ford was able to survive the crisis. The car was the basis for a series of large and strong cars that were made until the 1950s. The Ford V8 was made from 1932 until 1952.

08

09

10

11

12

13

14

15

Madcap races

There were many endurance races during the early days of the motor car that were intended to test the reliability of the cars. The Le Mans 24 hour race and the 1,000 mile Mille Miglia were in no way exceptional. Races could be far more severe. The most difficult tests were the Peking-Paris and the Carrera Panamerica. This latter competition was from the south to the north of Mexico and became known as 'the death race'.

The Alfa Romeo is prepared for the Mille Miglia for veteran cars. It also competed in the original race.

The fine lines of this 108 series Alvis (from the late 1950s) exudes the sterling qualities for which the Alvis was renowned.

Alvis (Great Britain)

The Briton T.G. John and the Frenchman P.H. de Fréville founded the company T.G. John Ltd. in 1919. The name was changed to Alvis Car & Engineering in 1921. Throughout its life (the company was taken over by Rover in 1967) the Alvis name stood very high quality cars of fine styling, that endured.

It is still possible to see a Alvis on the road in Britain because of the exceptionally high quality construction of these cars.

16

17

18

19

20

21

22

23

The grill with vertical lamella is characteristic of MGs from the Sixties.

August

The speed record

People have always wanted to be the fastest. By the time of the arrival of the car it was possible to measure how fast someone travelled. During the twentieth century countless people have attempted to break the speed record; many failed, some with deadly consequences. The record was held by Frenchmen until 1905, then by British drivers until the Americans decided to win it and determined to keep it for themselves. Some extremely unusual cars have been built to break the record. For the high speeds needed today, rocket and jet engines are used.

During the Second World War, Willy's Overland developed a lightweight all-terrain vehicle with four-wheel drive. Ford built thousands of the 'Jeeps' under licence. The name arose from the way soldiers said the abbreviation 'G.P'. which stood for 'General Purpose'. They were also sometimes called Willy after their designer. After the war, the Jeep saw service in the armed forces of many countries. Other organisations such as fire brigades also used the Jeep.

24

25

26

27

This sportive Alfa Romeo proves that there is no need to break records or bones in order to enjoy speed in a classy car.

28 29 30 31

DAF 600 with opposed twin cylinder 590cc engine.

SEPTEMBER

1938 MG TA Roadster
(acrylic by Huub Lepelaar)

Trabant (former East Germany)

After the wall was opened up in 1989, it was not only East Germans that engulfed West Berlin. Television pictures showed thousands of Trabants on the streets. They looked incongruous because of a design that dated from the late 1950s. The car's concept originated from the type 90 DKW that came into Russian hands at the end of the war. After a long delay, production was started by a state owned enterprise based in Zwickau in 1958. The Trabant was never popular in the West with its put-put-putting two-stroke engine. It was quickly left behind in terms of the western notion of mobility, speed, and luxury. There was no choice other than the Trabant for the inhabitants of the former East Germany. They could not choose from the wide selection available to western consumers. Before buying a car, they first had to be patient on the waiting list.

Although the Trabant was made right up to the last days of the German Democratic Republic, it has now become a classic car. Following the reunification of Germany, former East Germans changed over as quickly as they could to western models. The enthusiasts for the Trabant are attracted to it because it represents a former era and culture that has gone. They even cherish the put-put sound of its two-stroke engine.

Peugeot (France)

Armand Peugeot started with cycles and made his first unsuccessful car in 1888/1889. That failure was a three wheeler steamer. After this he directed his attention towards the petrol engine. In 1898, the company became registered as Societé Anonyme Automobiles Peugeot. The well-known lion was the factory's emblem. A famous car from these early days is the 'Bébé Peugeot' of 1912. This was designed by Ettore Bugatti, who later set-up his own company.

The company merged with Citroën in 1976 and it purchased the European arm of the American Chrysler company (France, Spain, and Great Britain) in 1978. Chrysler Europe was amalgamated with the French company and its brands – Chrysler, Matra, Simca, and Sunbeam – were renamed Talbot in 1979. Peugeot is currently the largest European car manufacturer and probably the only such concern in the world where the majority of shares are controlled by the family.

Although this 1974 V6 automatic Peugeot looks in excellent condition, it has not run for two years.

The 'Automobiles Charron' marque was created in 1906 when British investor Davison Dalziel bought C.G.V. company founded by Fernand Charron, Léonce Girardot, and Emile Voigt who were successful drivers of the famous Panhard & Levassor cars. Charron became famous for winning the Gordon Bennett Cup in 1900. They began making their own cars in 1901, and these were also made under licence in the United States and Great Britain. The golden era for Charron cars was pre 1914. After the First World War the company sank into oblivion and was bought in 1930 by Farman. This 1914 Charron Charronette has a 845 cc four cylinder engine giving 10 horsepower and a top speed of 40 m.p.h. (65 k.p.h.).

05

06

The VW Beetle was the West German equivalent of the Trabant. Whilst the Trabant remained undeveloped, the Volkswagen was continuously improved. Long after the last Beetle was made in the Federal Republic, the Trabant continued to be produced in the Democratic Republic.

07 08 09 10

11 12 13 14

Triumph Spitfire (1978). The Spitfire, launched in 1962, was a successful model for Triumph. This Spitfire has a 1,500cc four cylinder engine, four gear rations plus an overdrive and a top speed of 100 m.p.h. (160 k.p.h.). This car has visited the whole of Western Europe in the 87,500 miles (140,000 km) it has been driven. After restoration, it was slightly faster than the car was new. The hood, seating, and trim are original, which is astounding for a car of this vintage.

Classic car shows

Veteran and classic car clubs and other motoring organisations regularly plan opportunities for spectators to enjoy these old cars. The owners take part gladly – part of their pleasure is derived from others admiring their cars. Sometimes it is possible to see cars being driven at shows, in rallies, or even at race meetings. Otherwise, classic cars are frequently on show both in or out of doors. Those who make the effort to visit such events are likely to be rewarded by seeing some of the most attractive classic cars.

15

16

17

18

Occasionally you come across a really magnificent example at a show. This exceptionally fine Jaguar XK120 was seen at the 1995 Essen Motor Show.

Jaguar Mk. II

Shows and rallies are usually buzzing with enthusiasts. With patience it is possible to find time to get to see the cars properly and to photograph them.

1961 Skoda Felicia. During the years of the People's Republic, Skoda also made sports cars of a type not regarded as socialist. Even more remarkable is that not all these cars were exported. Many of these Skodas were sold within the former Czechoslovakia.

19

20

23

24

27

28

Skoda (former Czechoslovakia)

The main establishments of Skoda are in Prague and Pilsen. The company has produced both cars and weapons for many years. The first Skoda car was made in 1925 as a Skoda-Hispano-Suiza. Prior to this the factory built cars under licence in another name. The company continued to construct and export cars to the West after the communists gained power, because money was desperately needed. After the fall of the iron curtain, the company's fortunes looked bleak with the opening up of its market to Western models of car. The company now looks firmly established as part of Volkswagen.

A 1961 'socialist' Skoda Felicia. This particular Skoda bore the addition of Super due to the addition of such luxuries as sun visors.

Alfa Giulietta Spider

21

22

25

26

29

30

The marque with the trident as its emblem was founded by the four Maserati brothers in 1914. After 1926, the company directed its entire efforts towards motor racing. Although the company's activities broadened again to a wider public when Adolfo Orfi took over the company in 1937, a Maserati continued to be a very exclusive car. This strategy proved unsound and Orsi had to sell Maserati in 1968. It was taken over by Allesandro de Tomaso.

A 1967 Maserati Mistral.

OCTOBER

1930 Morgan
(acrylic by Huub Lepelaar)

That some classic cars are less exclusive and more readily available can be an advantage. The owner of an MG or Triumph has considerably less difficulty finding spare parts than the owner of this Skoda Felicia. Spares for his car are expensive or not available. Those considering buying a classic car need to bear this in mind.

The classic car enthusiast will encounter an enormous variety of terminology. With the veteran cars there are descriptions such as 'Landaulette' and also 'Voiturette' which is broadly comparable with 'Runabout' used for a small open car or vehicle. Such names gradually disappeared and were replaced in the 1930s by descriptions such as 'Roadster' which meant an open two-seater, which later became known as a sports car, and undefinable names like 'Tourer' and 'Special'. Those determined to become involved with veteran and classic cars should become familiar with the meaning of all these terms.

1903 Lanef La-Croix
Little is known about the Lanef La-Croix make. The company was also known as Lacroix de Laville, and it made three wheeled cars between 1901 and 1904. The chassis and mudguards of this car are of wood. The single cylinder 699 cc motor was made by De Dion-Bouton and has a power of 6 h.p. The engine's power was transferred to the left rear wheel through a belt.

01 02 03 04

05 06 07 08

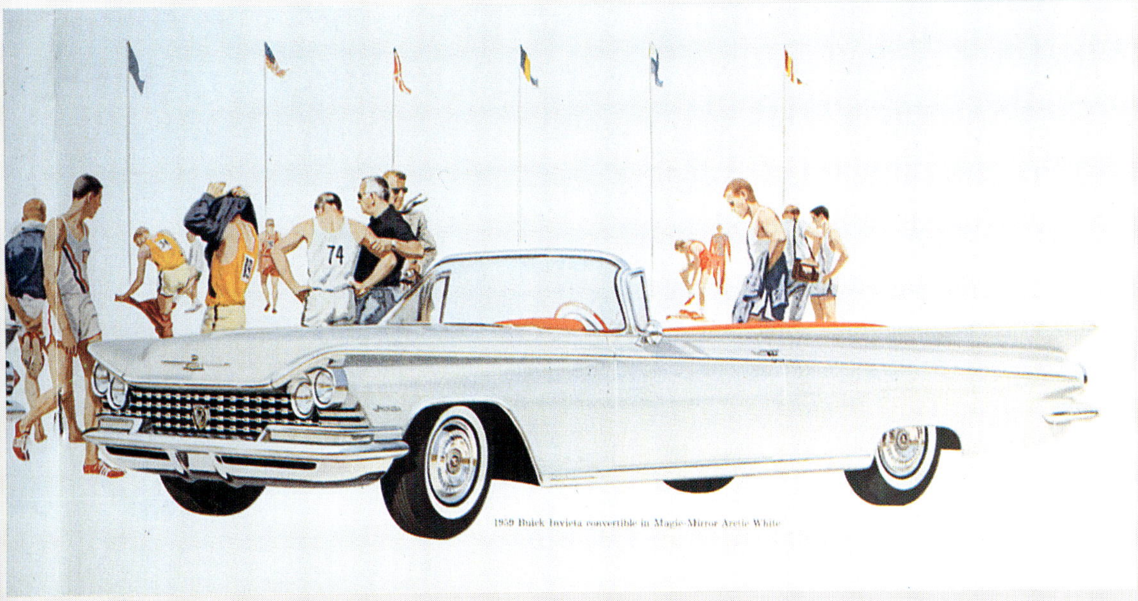

1959 Buick Convertible Invicta in 'Magic Mirror Arctic White'.

October

09

10

11

12

13

14

15

16

One of the parts made by Fiat is included in the name of this car – the Fiat 124 Spider Abarth. A competition prepared version of this car with a bigger engine won the Monte Carlo Rally along with other successes.

Fiat (Italy)

F.I.A.T. (Fabbrica Italiana Automobili Torino) came into existence in 1899 through the take over of the Ceirano car company by a group of engineers and financiers led by Giovanni Agnelli. Since that time Fiat has grown beyond imagination. In the course of time, Fiat took over Lancia, Itala, and S.P.A. and merged with OM. Abarth, Autobianchi, and Ferrari also belong to Fiat. A number of other companies also build Fiats under licence, such as Volga in Russia.

The Fiat 500 does not have outstanding performance yet it can still be regarded as a leading model, having perfectly captured the bottom of the market.

1911 Daimler Touring: four cylinders, 4,165 cc, 25 h.p. This car has the Silent Knight engine which has discs which perform the task of inlet and exhaust valves.

In its early years, the Alfa Giulia was an exclusive car. With twin overhead camshafts and sports-like but functional styling, it steadily gain a growing group of enthusiasts. A nice touch is the grab handles mounted on the rear door posts that were only installed for two years.

Lancia

The history of Lancia stretches back for almost a century. In 1906, Vincenzo Lancia set up his own business after a successful racing career with Fiat. The cars that he built were given a letter from the Greek alphabet. This model definition ended for a time following Vincenzo's death in 1937 with the Lancia Lamda. In the interim period the cars were given classical names such as Augusta and the Flaminia. The take over by Fiat in 1971 led to significant changes and Fiat let a new series of models to be designed. By the start of the 1970s, the marque's long experience in motor sport was able to find an outlet.

17

18

19

20

21

22

The Alfa Giulia was launched in 1962 as the successor to the Giulietta. The Giulia remained available until 1977as the Nuova Super (which appeared in 1974). This Alfa Giulia Super 1600 was built in 1971.

The fine classical lines from the 1950s give this Lancia a distinguished appearance.

1904 Spijker Double Phaeton

The post-war Triumph 1800 Roadster continued the pre-war roadster tradition.

1904 Spijker Double Phaeton. Maximum power 16 h.p. from a four cylinder 2,543cc engine. Spijker had great success in 1904 in events such as the Filey Sand Races and Brighton Speed Trials, held in Britain, where they gained a number of gold and silver medals. A feature of this Spijker is an entirely steel chassis. The steel bottom plate protected the passengers – many vehicles had no such protection against dust and dirt. The Double Phaeton therefore gained the nick-name of 'The Dustless Spijker'.

23

24

25

26

27

28

29

30

31

NOVEMBER

Ferrari 250 GTO
(acrylic by Huub Lepelaar)

The classic Alfa lines are seen in this Alfa Romeo 2000 GTV. If the car is compared with the superb Alfa Mille Miglia on the right, there appears to be little comparison. Yet this 2000 GTV has really benefited from the technical knowledge gained in developing the Mille Miglia Special. Alfa Romeo did not compete with their cars just for the publicity, but also to enable the experience gained to be utilised in their production cars.

Right: a marvellous 1,600cc engine that is the pride and joy of its owner gleams under the small oval bonnet.

MG A (1960), 1,600cc. This superb red sports car is ready for the grand tour. An appropriate leather case shines on the luggage rack. The MG A formed the bridge between the traditional MG models such as the MG TD and the more modern, extremely popular MG B. Note the fine curving lines and the reduced height radiator grill. The door can only be opened from inside. The piped edges to the seats and trim should be in the same colour as the bodywork.

Left: 1972 Mercedes 600 Pulmann

This 1948 Alfa Romeo Mille Miglia Special has a 2,500cc six cylinder engine and was built especially for the famous 1,000 mile race.

Note the characteristic half-height grill and the small oval bonnet or hood.

09

10

11

12

This imposing Lancia was used during the war by the Italian army as a staff car.

1971 MG Midget, 1,275cc. This compact extremely light tearaway of around 700kg is true to its name. Yet this midget among MGs should not be under estimated. It has a top speed of 97 m.p.h. (155 k.p.h.) and always does well in classic races and rallies. The Midget has a long history behind it going back to the Austin Healey Sprite of 1958. Many characteristics of the Sprite are retained in the Midget, such as the rounded shape beneath the front wing. This Midget is part of a rare series. Most Midgets have angular wheel arches. The Mark IV series by comparison has rounded rear wheel arches.

13 14 15 16

America and the automobile

The wide spread use of the motor car was much faster in the United States than in Europe. This was partly due to the Model T Ford, which made a consumer item out of a motor car. Statistics from 1931 show how far behind America Europe was (which also meant that it was an enormous potential market). In 1931 there was one car per four and a half head of population in the United States. The next highest country after America was Monaco with one car per fifteen inhabitants. The main industrial countries of Europe were a long way behind. France had 1/28, Great Britain 1/29, and Germany only 1/92. Smaller countries such as Belgium, The Netherlands, and Switzerland were around 1/50.

17 18 19 20

Chevrolet 31 Apache Pick-up. In contrast with the US, pick-ups are fairly rare in Europe. This Chevrolet Apache is therefore an unusual example.

November

Ferrari

After the experience of his own racing team, Enzo Ferrari started his own business in 1945. He concentrated himself totally on racing cars, sports cars, and grand tourers. Throughout the years, Ferrari has built the finest cars that always used the latest technological developments. The factory in Maranello did not produce large volume: never more than 400 per year. This has kept the marque exclusive. Although Ferrari now belongs to Fiat, the company has never wavered from its course. Ferrari therefore not only has a lasting image, the cars are also unobtainable for most people.

Ferrari 250 TDF (Tour de France)

Ferrari 250 GTB

21

26

This extremely unusual MG SA originates from 1937.

When the MG B was launched it turned out to have a monocoque body. The MG A enthusiasts were extremely disappointed because, according to them, this made the 'Roadster' far too comfortable. This was no longer a sports car! The disappointment was even greater when the MG B GT arrived on the market. This had nothing left of the sports car...

22 23 24 25

27 28 29 30

MG A Coupé

DECEMBER

1911 Opel
(acrylic by Huub Lepelaar)

Inset: The Bentley S3 Continental Saloon. In 1964 the car cost about £24,000, comparable with the price of a Rolls-Royce Silver Cloud, Mercedes-Benz 600, or a Ferrari 330GT. Bentley started the S-series in 1955, which was originally fitted with a V6 engine. The 6,320cc engine gave this Bentley a top speed of 119 m.p.h. (190 k.p.h.).

The racing examples from the Mille Miglia speak for themselves.

01

02

03

04

The Mille Miglia was a classic race. No one reached the finish without a first class car.

Although they appear to have nothing in common, the Renault Alpine A110 would never have existed without the experience gained by Renault with the 4CV.

Mercedes-Benz (Germany)

Mercedes Benz
220S Cabriolet

Mercedes-Benz was created by the merger of Mercedes (Gotlieb Daimler's company) and the company of Karl Benz. The name Mercedes came from the daughter of a banker who raced Daimlers. The three-pointed Mercedes emblem first appeared in 1909. Mercedes-Benz has established a name for keeping abreast of the latest technological innovation and for very solid, reliable, and fast cars. The Mercedes-Benz 220S Convertible above exudes the technical perfection of this German company.

05

06

07

08

Aston Martin 15/98 Speed Tourer of 1938. The Aston Martin name is derived from the surname of its founder (L. Martin) and his first racing success at the Aston Clinton hill climb in 1913. Aston Martin became a major name in racing but this cost so much money that the company became bankrupt in 1926. The business continues to exist, still under the same name, but it has changed hands a number of times. The image of very quick motor cars remains though. The 1,950cc four cylinder engine of this Aston Martin Speed Tourer delivers 110 h.p. and takes the car to a top speed of 96 m.p.h. (154 k.p.h.).

Buick (United States)

Buick was founded in 1903 by David Buick, who was one of the leading figures in the formation of General Motors. The cars from the factory bearing his name became known as solid, luxurious cars, for a reasonable price. Buick were known for the limousines they built in the 1930s and for the large coupés from the 1950s. A sample of the cars from the later years also gives a good impression of Buick through the years.

09 10 11 12

13 14 15 16

1956 six seater Buick Roadmaster, 2 door Riviera model 76R, 127 inch wheelbase, 255 h.p.

1956 six seater Buick Roadmaster Convertible model 76C, 127 inch wheelbase, 255 h.p.

In the years after the war, BMW did not make the powerful cars for which it is now well known. The demand at the time was for small inexpensive transport. For this market, BMW built the Isetta 300 three-wheeler. This example was built in 1957. The door is at the front of the car. To make room for getting into the car, the steering was hinged so that it could be folded back with the door.

Alfa Sprint 1600

Alfa Romeo (Italy)

Alfa Romeo came into existence when the firm of Alfa was taken over by Nicola Romeo. Alfa Romeo has always built fast cars. That was true of both the production cars and the racing cars. Racing was always a way to gain publicity. The company was very successful in this matter – before and after the war, their racing cars were legendary. After it became part of Fiat, Alfa Romeo took no more part in motor sport.

The red cross and biblical serpent of the Milanese crusaders form the emblem of Alfa Romeo.

Alfa 2600 Zagato

17 18 19 20

21 22 23 24

1906 Wolseley Siddeley, four cylinder, 3,300cc, 18 h.p. with four gear rations. This Wolseley was one of the first limousines. The chauffeur sits unprotected behind the wheel whilst the passengers are in a closed off cabin.